CREEPY CRAWLIES

Feasting Bedbugs, Mites, and Ticks

Carrie Gleason

Crabtree Publishing Company

www.crabtreebooks.com

CREEPY CRAWLIES

Developed and produced by
Plan B Book Packagers

Author:
Carrie Gleason

Editorial director:
Ellen Rodger

Art director:
Rosie Gowsell-Pattison

Logo design:
Margaret Amy Salter

Editor:
Molly Aloian

Proofreader:
Crystal Sikkens

Project manager:
Kathy Middleton

Production coordinator
& prepress technician:
Katherine Berti

Photographs:
Centers for Disease Control and Prevention: Public Health
   Image Library (PHIL): p. 8 (bottom right)
Rosie Gowsell: p. 27 (bottom)
Istockphoto: Cerobit: p. 24 (bottom); dblight: p. 6 (top);
   ToddMedia: p. 22
Photos.com: cover, logo
Shutterstock: cover, p. 1–2; Galyna Andrushko: p. 12 (bottom);
   Anson0618: p. 25 (top and bottom); Cheryl Casey: p. 5 (bottom);
   Kristof Degreef: p. 3, 24 (top); eAlisa: p. 16; Four Oaks:
   p. 13 (bottom); Jeffrey M. Frank: p. 20; Karel Gallas: p. 13 (top);
   Gary718: p. 19 (bottom); Benjamin Haas: p. 26 (bottom);
   Amy Nichole Harris: p. 27 (top); Jiri Haureljuk: p. 12 (top);
   Gabrielle Hovey: p. 9 (bottom); Brendan Howard: p. 10 (top);
   injun: p. 25 (middle); iNNOCENt: p. 18 (bottom); Sebastian
   Kaulitzki: p. 4 (top), 10 (bottom), 26 (top); Falk Kienas:
   p. 23 (top and middle right); D & K Kucharscy: p. 11 (right),
   15 (top); Doug Lemke: p. 5 (bottom); Liane M: p. 21 (bottom);
   Rob Marmion: p. 21 (top); Mats: p. 23 (left); Terence Mendoza:
   p. 9 (top); Robert Naratham: p. 29 (bottom); Denis Nata:
   p. 18 (top); nazira_g: p. 7; Netfalls: p. 8 (left), 19 (top);
   Reddogs: p. 28 (bottom); Smit: p. 6 (bottom); Alex Staroseltsev:
   p. 28 (top); Artur Tiutenko: p. 15 (bottom); Tobik: p. 14;
   WitR: p. 11 (left), 13 (middle); Zoom Team: p. 29 (top);
   Zurijeta: p. 4 (bottom)

Library and Archives Canada Cataloguing in Publication

Gleason, Carrie, 1973-
    Feasting bedbugs, mites, and ticks / Carrie Gleason.

(Creepy crawlies)
Includes index.
ISBN 978-0-7787-2500-8 (bound).--ISBN 978-0-7787-2507-7 (pbk.)

    1. Bedbugs--Juvenile literature. 2. Mites--Juvenile literature.
3. Ticks--Juvenile literature. 4. Mites as carriers of disease--Juvenile
literature. 5. Ticks as carriers of disease--Juvenile literature.
I. Title. II. Series: Creepy crawlies (St. Catharines, Ont)

QL523.C6G54 2010   j595   C2010-901756-0

Library of Congress Cataloging-in-Publication Data

Gleason, Carrie, 1973-
 Feasting bedbugs, mites, and ticks / Carrie Gleason.
     p. cm. -- (Creepy crawlies)
 Includes index.
 ISBN 978-0-7787-2500-8 (reinforced lib. bdg. : alk. paper)
 -- ISBN 978-0-7787-2507-7 (pbk. : alk. paper)
 1. Mites as carriers of disease--Juvenile literature. 2. Ticks as carriers of
disease--Juvenile literature. 3. Bedbugs--Juvenile literature. 4. Mites--Juvenile
literature. 5. Ticks -Juvenile literature. I. Title. II. Series.

 RA641.M5G54 2011
 614.4'33--dc22   2010009552

Crabtree Publishing Company

www.crabtreebooks.com   1-800-387-7650

Printed in China/072010/AP20100226

Published in Canada
Crabtree Publishing
616 Welland Ave.
St. Catharines, Ontario
L2M 5V6

Published in the United States
Crabtree Publishing
PMB 59051
350 Fifth Avenue, 59th Floor
New York, New York 10118

Published in the United Kingdom
Crabtree Publishing
Maritime House
Basin Road North, Hove
BN41 1WR

Published in Australia
Crabtree Publishing
386 Mt. Alexander Rd.
Ascot Vale (Melbourne)
VIC 3032

Contents

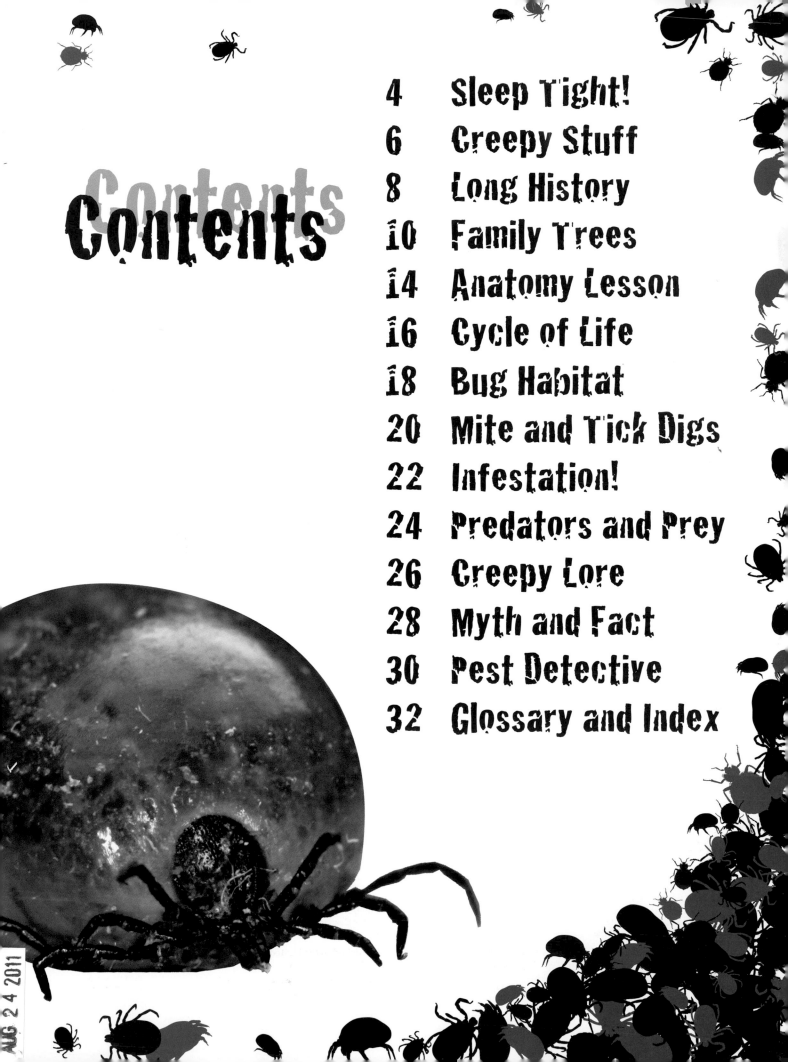

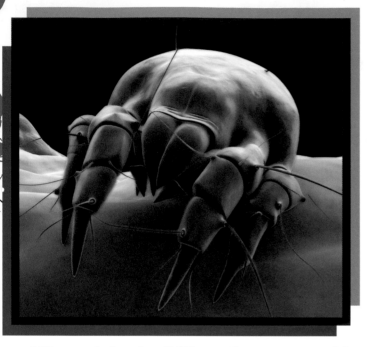

Mites eat dander. Without them, we would be wading through piles of dead skin much thicker than this man's dandruff.

Have you ever had the icky sensation that your skin is crawling? Does it feel like tiny little bugs are scampering over your arms, your legs, and your face? Well there really may be bugs on you—ones that are too small for you to see.

The "Invisible" Bug

That's right! These bugs are so small that they can only be seen with a microscope. They are all over you, your chair, your bed, and the floor, too! These tiny bugs are called mites, and there are over 40,000 known **species**. In fact, scientists believe there might be up to one million different species! One of the most common mites affecting humans are dust mites, which feed on dander, or dead flakes of skin.

Creatures of the Night

That's not all. You might also be horrified to learn that there are tiny bugs that suck your blood while you sleep. Bedbugs are large enough to be seen without a microscope, but too clever to be found. These bugs come out in the dead of night for only short periods of time to feast on your blood.

"I Vant To Drink Your Blood"

Many insects live off other animals. One **organism** that lives off another is called a parasite. Bedbugs are human parasites. Ticks, eight-legged creepy crawlies that are closely related to mites and spiders, are also parasites. Ticks spend their whole lives waiting for a **host** to feed on. Most times ticks prefer animals such as dogs, deer, or birds, but sometimes they feed on human hosts.

Revenge of the Parasites

Mites, bedbugs, and ticks have been around for a long time. But in the last ten years, these tiny pests have become an increasing problem for humans.

Ticks swell up after feeding on a host's blood.

CRAWLY FACT

Are You Creeped Out Yet?

Does the thought of little bugs terrify you? If so, you may be suffering from entomophobia—the irrational fear of bugs or insects. The letters "ent" come from the Greek word for "insect," while phobia means "to fear." Or maybe it's not the bugs themselves that bother you, but the idea of them feeding off of you? An unfounded fear of this type is called "delusional parasitosis."

Creepy Stuff

A bedbug is smaller than a grain of rice and its waste (that tiny white speck to the left of the bug) is even smaller.

Some mites live on human eyelashes.

There are two main types of parasites. Ectoparasites live on the outside of the body. Endoparasites live inside the body. Almost all animals are host to some sort of parasite. Scientists believe it's an important part of the food web.

Unwanted Guests

Most parasites are small invertebrates. Invertebrates are soft-bodied animals such as worms and insects. Parasites do not have skeletons inside their bodies so they can easily squeeze into small spaces to hide. They need to be able to get on (or in) their living, moving hosts, and stay on for the ride. Parasites are surprisingly well **adapted** to their hosts. It's like they were made for one another.

Human Parasites

There are about 430 different types of parasites that live off humans. Luckily, we aren't **infested** by all these at once! Bedbugs and some species of mites are two types of human ectoparasites. There are as many as 108 species of bedbugs, but only three are known to feed off human blood. The others are parasites of birds and bats. Mites are small, and range from the largest of the species—about the size of a walnut—to the smallest, about 0.001 inches (.03 mm) long. There are 30 to 40 different types of mites that can affect humans. Some survive by feeding off blood. Others, like dust mites and eyelash mites, feed off dead skin cells.

What Makes Them Bad?

Other than the gross-out factor, there are negative effects of living with parasites. Bedbug bites can be painful, and cause welts to rise up on the skin. Dust mites themselves don't harm humans, but their waste causes **allergic** reactions in some people. But ticks pose the greatest danger. They are known to spread diseases to humans. Parasites that carry diseases, are called vectors.

Stuffy in the morning? Maybe you are reacting to dust mite waste in your enviroment.

Creatures of the Night

Parasites do their best to stay hidden and to stay alive. For some species, that means being active only at night. Bedbugs bite when we are sleeping. Scabies are mites that burrow under human skin and lay their eggs there. The eggs cause an allergic reaction, which makes the area itch. When the eggs hatch, the new scabies live in the burrows under the skin until they grow into adults. The itch is worse at night, when the mites are moving around.

Long History

As far as scientists can tell from **fossils**, mites have been around for about 380 million years. Bedbugs have been around for about 325 million years. Ticks are the oldest of all. Scientists believe they emerged 450 million years ago.

Cave Sweet Cave

The earliest bedbugs were much larger and had wings. Originally, bedbugs were parasites of bats and birds. When prehistoric people slept in caves, they came into contact with the bugs. Humans have less hair and more exposed skin than bats and birds, so the bugs preferred living off humans.

Bedbug Afterlife

A fossilized bedbug has been found in an ancient Egyptian tomb that is believed to be 3,500 years old. That's older than **King Tut**! Ancient Romans and Greeks also had bedbugs. The bugs later migrated to colder climates. In **medieval** Europe, bedbugs affected the wealthier people who could afford to keep their homes warm and dry, which bedbugs prefer. People in ancient times also had scabies. Scientists estimate that scabies have infected humans for about 2,500 years, but because of the mite's size, no one knew what caused scabies. Most doctors believed that scabies were caused by an internal problem. In 1687, two Italian scientists discovered that the itch was caused by the *Sarcoptes scabiei* mite.

Egyptians wrote about bedbugs in their science books and plays. Archeological evidence of them has been found in mummies' tombs.

Land Ahoy!

European **colonists** brought bedbugs to North America on sailing ships. The ships were infested with the bugs, along with other parasites such as fleas and lice. By 1700, bedbugs had become a regular pest in North America's English colonies. One hundred years later, they had infested trains, hotels, and homes.

Fighting the Bugs

By 1900, about one-third of residences in large cities were infested. Central heating in homes, instead of wood-burning stoves or fireplaces, meant that houses could be kept at a constant warm temperature, so the bugs thrived year-round. People used all sorts of methods to get rid of them, but bedbugs remained a problem until a chemical **pesticide** called DDT became available in the 1940s. By the 1950s, bedbugs had nearly disappeared. While DDT had proved to kill bedbugs, it was also believed to kill birds and cause cancer. Because of this, DDT was banned in the United States in 1973. Nature also fought back. Within a few years, DDT-**resistant** bedbugs began to appear.

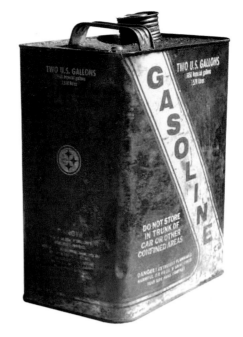

Early bedbug control methods included dousing beds in a mixture of boiling water, the poison arsenic, and the chemical sulfur. People also tried gasoline, kerosene, and alcohol.

Bedbugs, as the name suggests, are just that—bugs. "Bug" is a word for an insect that pierces and sucks. Mites, on the other hand, are not insects. They are members of the same animal family as spiders. Scientists believe there are up to a million different kinds of mites, many of which haven't even been named by scientists yet. Ticks are just one kind of mite.

What's in a Name?

Biologists like to classify things in a system called taxonomy. This system was first written in a book by Swedish scientist Carl Linnaeus in 1735. In the book, Linnaeus divided living things into groups called kingdoms. Humans, along with bedbugs, mites, and ticks, all belong to the Animalia kingdom.

Carl Linnaeus' classification system has changed since his time and is more scientifically accurate today.

There are many kinds of mites. The dust mites that inhabit the mattresses and furniture in your home are microscopic.

All In the Family

Bedbugs belong to the Animalia kingdom, which includes humans, bugs, spiders, and all other animals. Their phylum is Arthropoda, which includes bugs, spiders, and crustaceans. Their class is Insecta, which includes bees, ants, flies, and millions of other bugs. Bedbugs belong to the Hemiptera order of true bugs. Other members of this order include aphids, leafhoppers, assassin bugs, and thousands of other creepy crawlies with sucking mouthparts. In the bedbug family, Cimicidae, there are about 91 different kinds of these creepy crawlies.

Mites and ticks belong to the same family as spiders. The family is called Arachnida.

Like bedbugs, aphids are true bugs that belong to the Hemiptera order.

11

What's Eating You?

The common bedbug, with the scientific name *Cimex lectularius* is found all over the world. Another kind of bedbug, *Cimex hemipterus* is found in the tropics. *Leptocimex boueti* bedbugs live in West Africa and South America.

Mighty Mites

Although there are a whopping 45,000 known species of mites, scientists believe this may only be five percent of the number of mites in existence. That means there could be millions of different kinds of mites! Why is it so hard for scientists to determine the number of mite species? Many mites are simply too small to see!

They're Everywhere

Mites can live unnoticed almost everywhere. Mites are found in both soil and in water. But mites that are parasitic live off animals. Some mites that affect humans are dust mites, which feed off pieces of dead human skin, and demodex mites, which live in hair **follicles**, and even under human skin.

Some mites are too small to see with the naked eye, while others are larger. Some live in tropical areas and some in deserts.

Ticking You Off

There are about 850 different species of ticks. Some feed on particular hosts such as deer, dogs, sheep, or cattle. Some even prefer to feed on reptiles and amphibians. Others will feed on any host. These are known as opportunistic feeders. They are the most dangerous kinds of ticks because they can carry disease from one species of animal to another.

Sheep ticks feed on lambs, adult sheep, and even dogs or humans.

These ticks have gorged themselves on blood and are now hanging out on the ears and face of their host.

13

Anatomy Lesson

As you might have guessed from their family, ticks and mites share many physical similarities to spiders. The main one is that they all have eight legs. Bedbugs have six legs.

Mite vs. Spider

The biggest difference between mites and spiders is their body shape. Spiders have bodies made up of two parts: a thorax and an abdomen. The legs are attached to the abdomen. Mites have only one large, sac-like body part called an idiosoma, to which their legs are attached.

Hard Bodies vs Soft Bodies

When a tick feeds, its idiosoma expands as it fills with blood. A tick can more than double its size after feeding. Some ticks have a shield called a scutum that covers the backs of their bodies. These ticks are called hard ticks. Males have larger scutums than females, which prevents their bodies from expanding when they eat. This means that male ticks cannot take in as much blood as females. Males have to feed more often. Examples of species of hard ticks are dog ticks, deer ticks, and lone star ticks. Soft ticks don't have a scutum. Bird ticks are generally soft ticks.

Soft ticks are named for their soft, round exoskeletons.

Tick Bodies

A hard tick has a capitulum that sticks out at the front of its body. This is where the mouthparts are located. A soft tick's mouthparts are usually underneath its body.

Ticks have three main mouthparts for feeding. When a tick is ready to feed, two long sensing organs called palps open on the front of its head. Within the palps is a barbed, needle-like part called a hypostome.

The tick uses two fang-like parts called chelicerae to scrape away skin and make a hole to pierce the skin. Then feeding begins.

Ticks have hairy legs with claws on the end of them. The claws are perfect for grasping onto plant stems and animal hairs.

Their first pair of legs act as sensors to detect heat and carbon dioxide. This is because ticks have no eyes. Instead, the sensors tell them when a host is approaching.

Bedbug Bodies

A bedbug has a long, needle-like proboscis, or mouthpart. When ready to feed, the bedbug uses its proboscis to pierce the skin of its host. There are two tubes inside the proboscis. One tube injects the bedbug's saliva into the host. The other sucks the host's blood. The bedbug folds up its proboscis when it is finished feeding.

A bedbug has a flat, oval-shaped body. Like other insects, a bedbug has three body parts—a head, a thorax, and an abdomen. It does not have wings, but it has six legs.

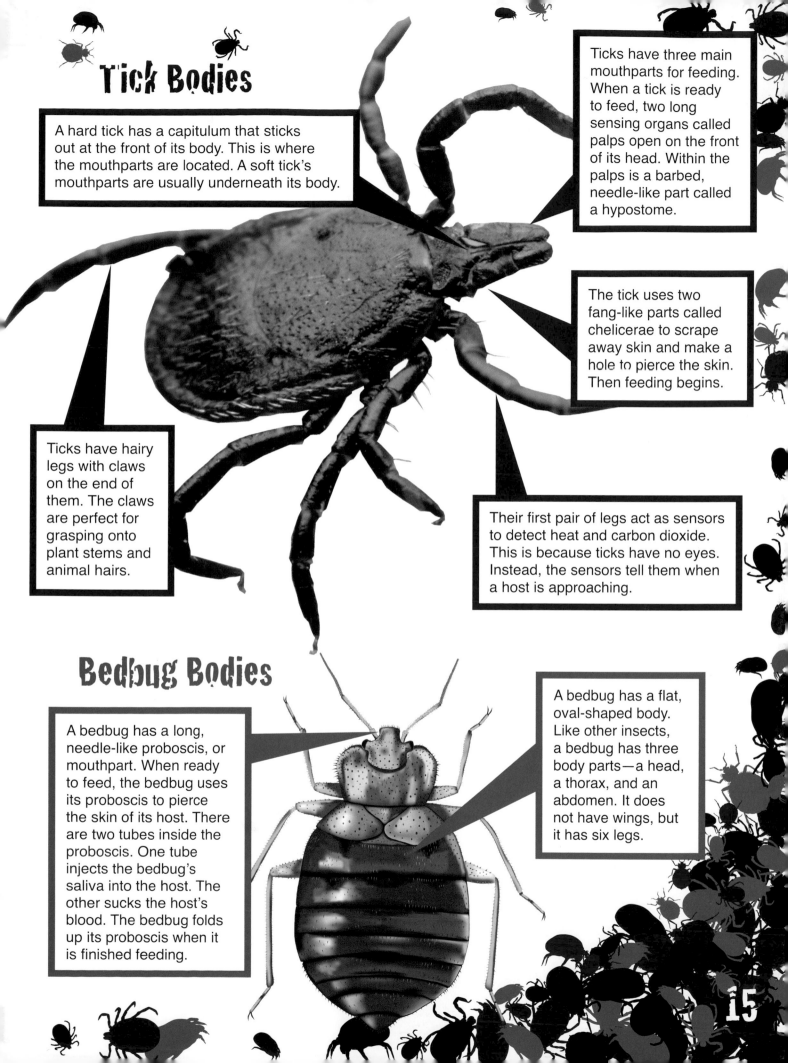

Cycle of Life

All insects and spiders, including bedbugs, mites, and ticks, begin life as eggs. They undergo a series of changes called metamorphosis before becoming adults. A complete life cycle, from egg to death, for bedbugs is about one year. It is less than a year to three years for certain kinds of ticks. Most mites live for 10 to 70 days. Bedbugs have three life stages, while mites and ticks have four or more life stages.

While feeding, the host animal may move away from where the seed tick first attached to it. This is how ticks travel large distances.

In the Beginning

A female bedbug can lay one to five eggs each day, or as many as 500 eggs in a lifetime. The eggs are deposited into cracks and crevices near a host's sleeping area and cemented there by a sticky paste. In one to two weeks, the eggs hatch. Some hard ticks lay as many as 10,000 eggs at once. Others lay 20 to 50 at a time. Tick eggs are usually deposited onto the ground.

Larvae

Ticks hatch into larvae, the first stage of their development. Tick larvae look similar to adult ticks, but have only six legs and are nearly impossible to see. The young tick, called a seed tick, must eat right away. It has to attach to a host and feed on blood in order to grow into its next life stage. After feeding, the seed tick drops off its host and molts. When invertebrates molt, they are shedding their **exoskeleton**, which has grown too small.

Tick life cycle

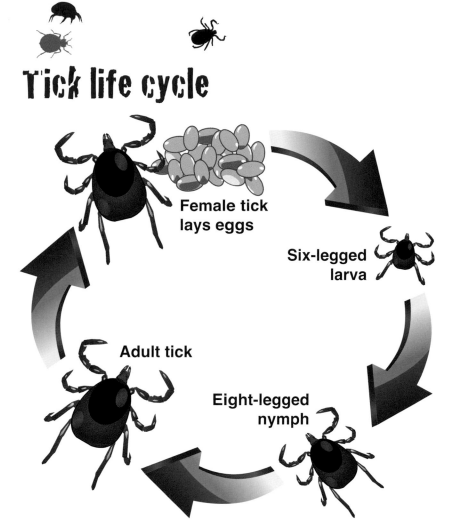

Female tick lays eggs

Six-legged larva

Eight-legged nymph

Adult tick

Bedbug life cycle

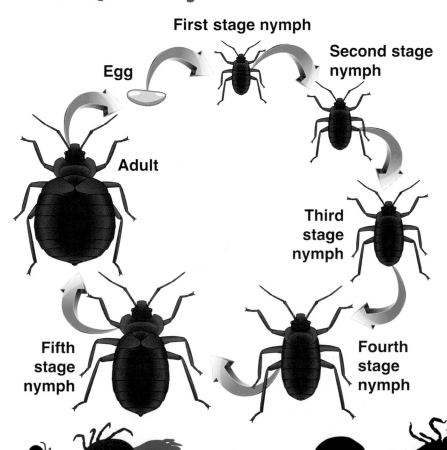

First stage nymph

Egg

Second stage nymph

Adult

Third stage nymph

Fifth stage nymph

Fourth stage nymph

Nymphs

After molting, the tick larva becomes a nymph. The nymph climbs up the stalk of a weed or long grass and waits for a host to pass by. Once it finds a host, the tick feeds for several days before dropping off and molting again. Bedbugs hatch from their eggs as nymphs. The nymph stage lasts from six weeks to several months, depending on the conditions. During this time a young bedbug molts five times, changing from a tiny, colorless insect to an adult. Between each molting, the bedbug nymph feeds on a host's blood for about five to ten minutes.

Adults

Adults are the last life cycle stage. Adult bedbugs live for six to twelve months. They spend their days hiding and digesting their meal from the night before. Adult ticks usually live for a year.

Bug Habitat

They're called bedbugs, but that doesn't mean they only live in beds. While bedbugs can be found in the seams and folds of mattresses and box springs, these pests will also hide out almost anywhere close to a sleeping person. Their flat bodies allow them to get into tight places, including cracks in walls, under loose wallpaper, or behind posters and pictures.

Ideal Conditions

Bedbugs don't have wings, so they can't fly from place to place. They can't jump either. They are fast runners, but they still prefer hiding to moving from place to place in search of food. They are sensitive to extreme hot or cold temperatures, so warm houses suit them best. If a bedbug lacks a human host, it can survive for up to a year without feeding, or it can feed on rodents, cats, or dogs.

Bedbugs may be lurking in bedding and mattresses, but they can hide anywhere, including in telephones.

Watch out Fido! If bedbugs can't find a human host, they'll munch on pets.

Traveling Bugs

There are two ways that bedbugs can find a new home. They can either "hitchhike," by crawling onto your clothing or into your bags and move with you wherever you go, or they can **migrate** to a new place. Migrating bedbugs simply walk to a new location. This is why buildings like hotels, hospitals, nursing homes, jails, and shelters are high-risk places for bedbug infestations. The bugs in these buildings travel hallways, pipes in walls, and electrical lines to find a host. A high occupancy rate means plenty of food for bedbugs, and once fed, they multiply quickly.

Bedbugs can "hitchhike," or find their way into a traveler's bags and move to new territory in luggage.

THAT'S CREEPY

Attack of the Pesky Bedbug

An attack of the bedbugs! In 2002, there were two reported cases of bedbugs in New York City. In 2004, there were 537 cases. Two years after that, in 2006, there were 6,889 reported cases. That's an increase of over 1,000 percent in just two years! And that number doesn't reflect all the people who were too embarrassed to call and report the bugs. The numbers continue to rise every year. In March 2009, New York finally created an advisory board of ten people who range from pest control professionals to health experts who will tell the mayor what to do to solve the problem.

Unlike bedbugs, ticks prefer life in the country. This is because their hosts are usually forest dwellers. Ticks like to hang around on the tips of plants and long grasses, waiting for an animal to pass by. This is called "questing." When a tick's sensory organs pick up the vibrations or shadow of a host, they wave their front legs frantically in the air, trying to grab hold.

Tickville

In wooded areas, ticks receive plenty of protection from the wind and the Sun. They receive the same wind and Sun protection in natural areas in cities, backyards, and beachfronts. They can come into contact with humans who are out walking on trails in the woods, or are passed from animals such as deer, birds, and rodents to people.

Ticks are common in many wooded areas.

Mite-y Home

Mites live in almost every habitat on Earth, including water and land. Some mites, like spider mites, live and feed off plants. These mites can cause **havoc** for farmers if crops such as soybeans or grains become infested.

Dust mites like to live in places where the temperature is between 65°F and 80°F (18°C and 27°C). This range of temperatures also happens to be what most home thermostats are kept at. Rooms with high humidity, or moisture, help the mites because the moisture in the air causes a mold to form that breaks down their food before they eat.

Humans shed about 40,000 skin cells per minute. Some of it gets brushed away as flakes. Dust mites in a home can be found in fabric-covered furniture, carpeting, mattresses, and inside bedsheets, blankets, and pillows.

CRAWLY FACT

Decomposers

Most species of mites are beneficial to humans. That's because mites break down organic, or once-living, matter. Good examples of decomposers are the mites that live in soil. They help break down plant matter to make rich soil for new plants to grow.

Some mites can live in compost piles.

Infestation!

It doesn't take much for mites, ticks, or bedbugs to move into an area where conditions are right. An infestation happens when a large number of unwanted pests inhabit a small area. Here are some ways to help you avoid an infestation, or deal with one if they do occur.

Tips and Ticks

Here are some tips to avoiding that creepy crawly feeling:

- To prevent bedbug bites, be careful when buying secondhand clothing or furniture. Avoid mattresses or furniture that have been sitting on the street.
- Check your bed for signs of bedbugs (black spots and skin casings). Turn your mattress monthly and make sure your bedsheets are washed in hot water and dried in a dryer if possible.
- Wear long pants when walking or hiking through wooded areas where ticks might be lurking.
- Purchase a thick plastic mattress cover that seals up tight. This will prevent the bedbugs living in your mattress from coming out to feed.
- Vacuum regularly to keep the dust mite population down. Steam cleaning carpets and furniture can also help.
- Diatomaceous earth is a powder made from tiny, sharp-pointed algae. Sprinkle this natural soil on the floor around the bed and near cracks. When the bedbugs pass over the earth, they will cut themselves and die.

An exterminator can get rid of bedbugs using insecticides.

Tick Removal

If you find a tick attached to you or to your pet, have tweezers on hand to remove it. Using the tweezers, grab the tick by its head and pull straight out until the tick comes off. Be careful not to twist or jerk the tick as this can cause its body to break away from its head. Do not grab the tick by its body and never try removing it using petroleum jelly, gasoline, or nail polish. These methods can cause the tick to inject bacteria from its stomach into the host!

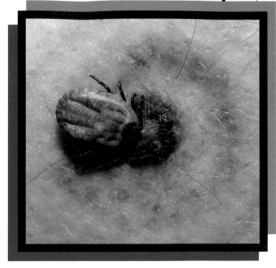

Tick's leave huge red welts. Removal can be tricky business.

An old mattress can contain up to 10 million dust mites! There are special mattress covers that encase the dust mites.

CRAWLY FACT

Lyme disease

Deer ticks are also called blacklegged ticks because of the color of their legs. They are especially dangerous for humans because they are vectors for Lyme disease. Lyme disease is caused by a bacteria called spirochete. When a human host is bitten by a nymph carrying the bacteria, the disease is passed on. Lyme disease affects the skin, joints, and nervous system. In mild cases, people with the illness will feel flu-like symptoms and develop a rash around the tick bite. The most severe cases lead to **paralysis**.

You wake up with three red, puffy bumps on your arm. You are breakfast, lunch, and supper for a bedbug. YOU are its prey.

Getting Down to Business

Bedbugs are so well-suited to suck human blood that we don't even feel their bites as they are happening. When a bedbug bites, one of the tubes in their mouthparts injects a saliva-like fluid into the wound. The fluid acts as an **anesthetic**, so that the host can't feel the bite. It also stops human blood from **clotting**, so the blood keeps flowing. Victims are left with red bite marks.

Tick Feeding

While bedbugs feed for about 15 minutes at a time, an adult female tick can feed for days. The female tick cannot let go until her body has finished feeding. Sometimes, a male tick will come along and pierce her bloated body and feed off of her. The male tick also fertilizes the female's eggs while she is feeding.

Ticks can become so engorged, or filled with blood, that their legs no longer touch the host.

Bedbugs can leave behind a lot of waste.

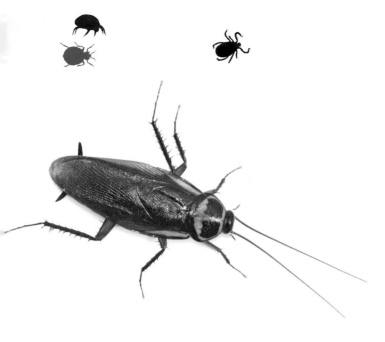

Insect Buffet

Unfortunately for humans, the predators of bedbugs are not any more welcome in our homes (or beds!) than bedbugs. Bedbug predators include cockroaches, house centipedes, masked assassins, and fire ants. In a particularly gruesome revenge on bedbugs, fire ants will attack, tear a bedbug apart, and carry the pieces back to their nest to eat. The downside? Fire ants will also bite humans!

Mite vs. Might

Some of the pests mentioned in this book are difficult to combat because scientists are unsure of their natural predators. Some scientists believe that micro-predators might prey on dust mites. Some mites are known to prey on larger mites, such as the spider mites that affect crops. Farmers and gardeners sometimes introduce these other types of mites to the crops to control the spider mite population. Scientists are not sure what preys on ticks. Some people raise chickens and guinea fowl in the hope that these birds will eat them.

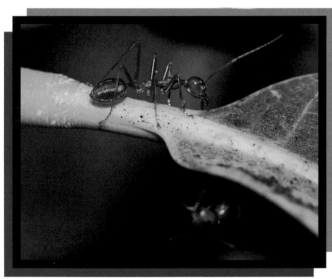

Fire ants and cockroaches are bedbug predators.

Creepy Lore

Although bedbugs, mites, and ticks have been around for a very long time, they haven't always been understood as well as they are today. The recent comeback these critters have made means that society and science have a renewed interest in learning about them.

SLEEPING TIGHT

The rhyming phrase "goodnight, sleep tight, and don't let the bedbugs bite" is still told to children before bedtime. But the meaning is almost lost. Some word experts, or etymologists (not to be confused with insect scientists, known as entomologists) believe the words "sleep tight" mean "sleep well." Others think "sleep tight" referred to a type of rope frame bed that people used to sleep in before mattresses were invented. The ropes needed to be tightened to carry the weight of sleeping people.

NAMING THEM

There are a lot of names given to bedbugs. From the Spanish word for bedbug comes the name chinch bugs. In the past, they were called wall lice, and even night crawlers. The name often reflected what people thought of the pests.

TICKED OFF?

Ticks have a place in our stories and sayings. The name "tick" can be used to refer to someone who is unpleasant. To say you are "as full as a tick," means you have eaten too much.

THE RED COATS

One of the names given to bedbugs in colonial America was "red coats." Bedbugs turn from a light brown color to dark reddish-brown after they have filled up on blood. Seems like a pretty suitable name, right? But there was another reason that the colonists gave them this nickname. The British had said that the bugs infesting England had arrived in wood from North America. Insulted, the Americans named the bugs "red coats" in reference to the red coats worn by the despised British soldiers.

UNLIKELY SUPERHERO

A comic book created in the 1980s and a television series in the 1990s featured an unlikely superhero called "The Tick." This tick hero had escaped from Evanston Asylum before beginning his career fighting crime. The Tick wasn't a very smart superhero, and if he lost his antennae, he would get dizzy and fall over.

MITEY MITE

People sometimes refer to young children as "mites" because they are small like mites. The word mite is also used to describe a small amount of something. Widow's mites are coins, or money that used to be given to widows and poor people.

A little kid is sometimes called a "mite."

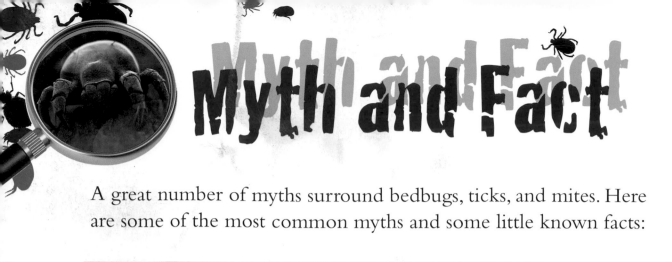

Myth and Fact

A great number of myths surround bedbugs, ticks, and mites. Here are some of the most common myths and some little known facts:

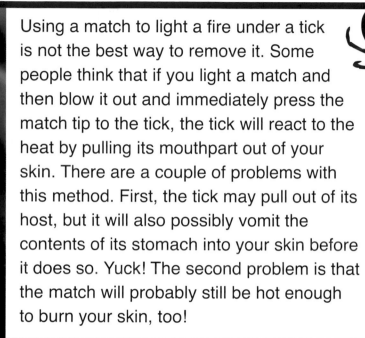

Using a match to light a fire under a tick is not the best way to remove it. Some people think that if you light a match and then blow it out and immediately press the match tip to the tick, the tick will react to the heat by pulling its mouthpart out of your skin. There are a couple of problems with this method. First, the tick may pull out of its host, but it will also possibly vomit the contents of its stomach into your skin before it does so. Yuck! The second problem is that the match will probably still be hot enough to burn your skin, too!

Flea and tick collars are used to prevent these insects from choosing your cat or dog as their host. Once a flea and tick collar has been put on an animal and activated (usually by pulling it), powdered pesticides cover the animal's fur. When the animal's coat and skin are covered, a flea or tick that grabs onto the host will be poisoned and killed. Eventually, the pesticide wears off, usually after about six months, and the treatment may need to be repeated.

Both bedbugs and dust mites are found in homes all over the world. Clean houses are not a guarantee that you will not be visited by either pest. Bedbugs love clutter, but they are brought into a home through exposure during travel (hotels), along electrical wiring and pipes, and from bringing secondhand furniture, clothes, and fabrics into the home. Dust mites are everywhere. They perform a function by eating our dead skin cells.

Eyelash mites are mites, unseen by the naked eye, that live in the follicles of our eyclashes. Other mites also live, eat, and breed on our eyebrows and around our noses. These Latin-named *Demodex folliculorum* and *Demodex brevis*, eat dead skin cells and **sebaceous** fluids. Under a microscrope, these mites look like worms with legs and claws. A lot of people have them, and they don't usually do any harm. Eyelash mites are more common on older people.

Scabies is an infection caused by a mite. Known in ancient times, it was sometimes called the seven-year-itch. In animals, it is called mange. The *sarcoptes scabiei* mite causes itchy rashes when it burrows under the skin to deposit eggs. Scabies can be easily transmitted from person to person through skin contact or through clothing, bedding, and towels. There are medical treatments that can get rid of scabies.

Pest Detective

Avoiding bedbugs, ticks, and mites is a good idea. But, if you see yourself as an entomologist, there are several ways for you to learn more about these creepy crawlies. Many universities have entomology departments that have displays of insects. Check their Web sites to see if these are open for public viewing. In addition, try these helpful Web sites for kids.

Here are some cool sites to check out:

Pestworld for Kids
www.pestworldforkids.org/guide.html
This is a great site for learning about insects of all kinds. Find pictures, read infosheets, get homework help, and play games. You can also learn fun science experiments that you can do at home.

Smithsonian Institution: BugInfo
www.si.edu/Encyclopedia_SI/nmnh/buginfo/start.htm
Look up different types of bugs and insects, and research special topics such as insect flight and bug hibernation. A list of science fair projects help you learn more and have fun.

Insects and Other Arthropods
www.kendall-bioresearch.co.uk/mite.htm
This site is a treasure trove of all things bugs and its mite section is mitey interesting! It is the Web site of an entomologist who teaches, writes, and consults about all things buggy.

KidInfo: Insects
www.kidinfo.com/Science/insects.html
This site is a great place to start research. It provides links and descriptions of other useful sites on insects, as well as photos and videos.

Here are some great books on mites, ticks, bedbugs and other insects:

The Insecto-Files, by Helaine Becker.
Toronto: Maple Tree Press, 2009.

What's Eating You?, by Nicola Davies.
Candlewick Press, 2008.

The World of Insects series.
Crabtree Publishing, 2005/6.

Big Book of Bugs and Other Creepy Crawlies
Dorling Kindersley, 2000.

Want to see bedbugs and ticks up close and personal? Here are some great places to visit:

American Museum of Natural History
Central Park West at 79th Street
New York, NY 10024-5192
Phone: (212) 769-5100

The Insect Zoo at San Francisco Zoo
1 Zoo Road
San Francisco, CA 94132
Phone: (415) 753-7080

Invertebrate Exhibit, The National Zoo
3001 Connecticut Ave., NW
Washington, DC 20008
Phone: (540) 635-6500

The O. Orkin Insect Zoo at the National Museum of Natural History, Smithsonian
10th Street and Constitution Ave., NW
Washington, DC 20560
Phone: (202) 633-1000

Glossary

adapted Adjusted or suited to certain conditions or environments

allergic Responses by the body's immune system to a foreign substance. This can mean anything from rashes to difficulty breathing and severe illness

anesthetic A substance that reduces pain

clotting Becoming thick

colonists A settler to an area

exoskeleton A hard external covering that provides support and protection for invertebrates

follicles The tissue that surrounds the roots of hair

fossils The remains of a prehistoric living thing preserved in rock

havoc Widespread disruption or disorder

host An animal on which a parasite lives

infested To overrun or be present in large numbers

King Tut An ancient Egyptian boy pharaoh

medieval From a period of history that spans 500 AD to 1100 AD

migrate To move from one region or habitat to another

molt Shedding a body or skin to make way for new growth

organism A life-form such as an animal or plant

paralysis Loss of the ability to move

pesticides Substances used for killing insect pests

resistant Immune or not vulnerable to something

sebaceous A small gland in the skin that secretes an oil that lubricates hair and skin

species A group of living things that have similar characteristics and are capable of interbreeding

Index